What the Angel Saw, What the Saint Refused

poems

George Franklin

Sheila-Na-Gig Editions

Cover photo: Hugo Simberg (1873–1917) Finnish
The Wounded Angel (1903), oil on canvas

ISBN: 9781962405041

Sheila-Na-Gig Editions
Russell, KY
Hayley Mitchell Haugen, Editor
www.sheilanagigblog.com

You will be astonished at what a narrative poem can achieve when you read George Franklin's ground-breaking collection, *What the Angel Saw, What the Saint Refused*. You will learn the difference between grief that is despairing and grief that is not despairing, the second hinging on an appreciation for the unremarkable life, as you follow an angel with no destination, an angel drawn by humanity's grief. *The angel can change nothing. / He is not here to bless or comfort, to join a war or stop one.* Still, capacious imagery challenges philosophy: *[pigeons] arc across the sky like missiles thrown off course,* and creates a beauty that transcends existentialist angst: *drafts / From the roof and door pulled the fire one way, then another.* The terrible beauty that exists, to borrow a phrase from Rilke, because Franklin's angel will make you think of Rilke, shows you that though *pain is never symmetrical,* your own grief will be balanced by a belief in something larger than death. You will find *harmony* in a *refuge of cellos* and resilience in *waking from a dream laughing.*

—Jane Ann Fuller, author of *Half-Life*

Acknowledgments

Many thanks to the editors and staff of the following journals in which these poems have appeared:

First Literary Review: "The Angel Looks for Harmony"
Solstice: "The Philosopher and the Angel"
The Banyan Review: "The Angel of Sorrow Considers Photography"
The Decadent Review: "Blasphemy," "During the War,"
  "Temptation," "The Dust of Books," "The Saint and the
  Gamblers," "The Saint of Unbelievers Visits the City," "The
  Voice of God," "To Believe in Nothing"
The Woven Tale Press: "The Saint of Unbelievers"

CONTENTS

Preface

It occurs to me that as not much narrative poetry is published these days, it might prove useful to describe how these two stories in poems came to be written. The angel first appeared in an earlier chapbook, *Travels of the Angel of Sorrow*. Those poems chronicled the angel's visit to a plague-ridden mountain village in winter. In *What the Angel Saw, What the Saint Refused*, the angel is drawn to suffering in other places and times, and as one of the poems describes, he has a habit of showing up in my living room and perusing my bookshelves. I am only partially joking. The angel poems, from the first, were written with little input from me. They were written quickly, and the editing was minimal. This was unlike any way I had ever written poetry before. I don't know who the "I" is that wrote them, but the "I" writing to you now at least knew enough not to interfere.

The poems of the saint of unbelievers were written the same way. I like the saint of unbelievers, although I'm pretty certain he wouldn't like me. I am his opposite: compromising, bourgeois, fond of companionship and creature comforts. I'm sure he would have preferred a better, more austere poet to write his story, but as my oldest son's kindergarten teacher used to tell her class: "You get what you get." As with the angel poems, I did not decide to write about the saint; the poems simply showed up.

If the angel of sorrow and the saint of unbelievers have something in common, it is that they both bear witness to suffering. Beyond that, their responses are entirely different. The angel doesn't know the purpose of his presence among humans, but grief draws him to itself repeatedly. He is helpless to improve matters, even though he sees what is happening with perfect clarity. The saint of unbelievers also refuses any subterfuge, excuse, or consolation that would diminish the harshness and injustice he witnesses. If the saint had been Job, he would have spit into the whirlwind or, better yet, laughed. He wants to shake people out of their certainties and especially rejects the transcendence of the philosophers. Unlike the angel, the saint sees a bitter humor in the tragedies that surround him, and that humor gives him an equanimity that surfaces in his conversations with the librarian. I was about to write "his friend the librarian," but I doubt the saint would admit to friendship.

Neither the angel nor the saint have any messages for anyone. They only have experience. Sometimes I wonder which of them most embodies negation: the angel who wants to understand but can't reconcile his understanding with the inevitable destruction or decay of all things, with contingency, or the saint who trains himself to reject any belief that would betray his knowledge of that same contingency and who even fears that the knowledge of death is itself a kind of belief. Regardless of such differences, they're both creatures of their own experience, and both, in very different circumstances, maintain their integrity.

I. What the Angel Saw

Not for the First Time

The angel of sorrow stares at a tank half-buried in snow,
The muzzle of its gun pointing down, ice crusting
Along the barrel. The hatch is open, and the cabin empty.

The angel can see tracks where soldiers ran into the forest,
The steam from their breath lost behind black tree trunks.
There is no traffic on the road, but there is a patch of ice,

Pink darkening to red. The angel notices that the sky is overcast,
And evening has already shadowed the horizon in the east.
Smoke rises in columns from the south. A city is burning.

Even though he knows that he could spread his wings
And be elsewhere, the angel stands still in the road.
Later, he will walk down a street that follows the curves

Of a river. In underground shelters, children are awake
Playing games on cell phones, while pigeons whose nests have been
Destroyed arc across the sky like missiles thrown off-course.

Air-raid sirens divide the night into before and after,
But the angel doesn't listen to them. From a footbridge,
He watches the fast-moving water and sharp edges

Of floating ice, uniforms caught on broken branches,
Explosions reflected in the current. The angel can change nothing.
He is not here to bless or comfort, to join a war or stop one.

If he hears cries, they are the same he heard at Béziers
And Jerusalem, Vicksburg and Stalingrad. A cloud moves
In front of the moon. It's better that no one sees him.

THE ANGEL OF SORROW MEETS HIS OPPOSITE

The meeting did not take place on top of a mountain or in the desert with looming sand dunes and a blue sky. They met on a busy street corner, near the museum where a market had stood a thousand years ago. It was raining, and they both wore large overcoats to conceal their wings.

Neither knew what to say to the other. The fallen one was too old for anger or snide remarks. Time moved through him like a wind coming off the sea. At first, they merely nodded, the courtesy of wrestlers before they enter the ring,

But the war they'd fought was over long before the waters had separated from the land or day from night. Traffic moved past them, car horns sounded, and tires sent run-off splashing back onto the curb.

The angel was the first to speak. I watch those who pass us here, and I read their lives, already written, read the innocence that clings to them, the futures they don't expect, the pasts they no longer remember. How have you lived with this for so long? How does the earth sustain the weight of such grief?

What you call grief, said the fallen one, is a terrible gift. Every day, I envy it. That street musician huddled beneath the canopy, his accordion covered in oil cloth to keep off rain— his voice creaks like the unoiled hinges on a church doorway, but no choir in heaven can echo the pain of those songs.

You and I, he said, were made for surmounting worlds, messengers who cross the indescribable. We are real in ways they are not, but unreal in ways they take for granted. They dole out time the way sultans gave whole villages to their janissaries, telling each other jokes and buying drinks. What is even a moment of such happiness worth?

The angel closed his eyes and saw the forest reclaiming sidewalks and office buildings, the city where they stood a silent ruin, the temporary graves, the glacier, and the coin someone dropped and never found.

The fallen one had been seduced by the beauty of finite things. The angel felt only their sorrow.

THE ANGEL LOOKS FOR HARMONY

Sometimes he stands at the back of the concert hall, listening as the horns and timpani come in, held in check by the conductor's extended hand. Then a quick nod to the woodwinds and the strings.

The angel is looking for harmony wherever he can find it. He takes refuge in cellos, violas, the double bass.

But from where he stands, he can see the king leaving the royal box. The concert is not half finished, but the king is leaving already. His entourage chats as they rise from their chairs—a lieutenant dressed in blue with gold braid and two ladies in waiting to the queen.

Later, one of the ladies in waiting, the blonde one who has not yet visited the king's chambers, claims she heard the flapping of wings.

The Angel of Sorrow Considers Photography

The angel is always surprised by photographs,
By how willing people are to reveal their faces,
Their slightest frowns, their lips holding back

A smile, satisfaction, cruelty, regret. He watches
As they open family albums, children in hot weather,
Sunburned noses and shoulders, an old woman almost

As small as they are, a man who hides his eyes
Behind dark lenses. The angel wonders
If they believe the photos will keep them safe,

Whatever happens, that they'll remain
At the birthday party, at the house in the mountains,
Or climbing onto the bus. How they want

To hold on to that happiness, the air they drink
Thoughtlessly, unaware of the blue veins
Under the skin of their palms, fragility of bone

And tissue. The angel also listens when they touch
Beneath their night clothes and blankets. He
Hears the breath leave their mouths, the creak

Of the bedframe beneath their weight. He sees
The imprint their bodies leave on the mattress.
This is also a photograph.

THE ANGEL OF SORROW DOESN'T RING THE DOORBELL

The angel of sorrow doesn't ring the doorbell.
He just appears, sometimes sitting in the green chair
With the stain on the left arm, sometimes standing,

Looking at the dog or studying my bookshelves.
I have to be careful because if I stare at him too long
The walls of the room fade, and I find myself

In Turin during a strike or watching Bolívar die,
Coughing in Santa Marta. It's better to sit and listen
As he tells a story—almost ignoring I'm here.

The stories he tells are for himself anyway. He takes
What he's seen and shapes it into words, stretching
Or folding so that sentences become a city with smoke

So dense men barely see each other, wounds
Covered by rags, buckets of urine emptied from windows,
Carriages pulled by black horses, and a scream

As a woman falls to the cobblestones.
He remembers the flowers blooming weirdly
At Hiroshima and a hillside at Antietam, the rows

Of bodies still in formation, broken stalks of corn,
Cavalry cleaning swords at St. Peter's Field,
Farms covered in dust, nothing left to eat

But canned tomatoes and gray flour, police firing
Into the dark at any shape that seems human.
The angel looks over at me, knows I've stopped listening.

This, he says, is what you wanted to see, isn't it? How it
Seems to end each time, a capital where the rulers
Sprinkle cologne on their hands and listen to violins—

Really good violins actually—and the musicians
And philosophers die of tuberculosis, syphilis, or shame?
I've learned it does no good to argue with the angel.

He refuses to admit that things are better now, or ever.
He looks at me sadly, perhaps with pity. He's seen
What happens to all of us.

THE ANGEL OF SORROW IS DRAWN TO A CITY

At night, behind a cluster of houses,
The angel sits on the branch of an oak tree.
He watches as television screens flicker

Through thin curtains or shades, as shadows
Move across the rooms. Above the balcony of
An apartment building, a couple is making love,

Their outlines barely visible. The angel
Did not decide to come here. To the east,
Office towers point accusing fingers

Up at heaven. Metal boxes shuffle
Along the roads and bridges. Their headlights
And grills remind him of cruel reptiles

Or birds of prey when they spy a rabbit.
Nearby, flat-roofed buildings are illuminated
Throughout the night. Figures enter and leave,

Carrying brown paper bags. To the angel,
These people seem on the verge of some
Burst of feeling, but whether it's anger, grief,

Or love he can't be sure. The angel dislikes
The smell of the metal boxes, but he watches
The larger ones cross the sky, red and green

Lights flashing some kind of incomprehensible
Promise. If he were asked to tell a story
About this place, he would describe a man

Speaking to a mirror, a woman crying beneath
A stream of hot water, a place with endless boxes,
More boxes than people, boxes of sounds, of

Lights, even of cold air in the summer. He flies
West over the empty spaces. The sorrow
Of cities pulls him to their rooftops.

He no longer tries to understand.

The Angel Is Always Interested in Explorers

The angel of sorrow is always interested in explorers.
They remind him of himself, except that if his own travels
Have a destination, he doesn't know it. He watches their ships
Set out with banners, official speeches, even a march
Composed for the occasion, crowds cheering until
Only a wavering line of smoke is visible where ocean
Meets the air. He knows they travel to unwelcoming places
No one else has wanted to visit, gaping deserts,
Ice-covered poles, jungles too remote even for exploitation.
He watches them sweat or freeze, reads the notebooks
Where they scratch last letters to wives and children,
To parents who'd imagined other futures for their offspring,
Honors easier to come by. Sometimes, they race to a spot
Only distinguished by a compass, dogsleds abandoned
Or ice cracking the ship's hull. Sometimes, they die there,
And he watches that as well: vomiting and fevers,
Swollen extremities, an incurable thirst, numbness
Ending in frostbite, their final thoughts speculation,
What might have happened if they'd hired different guides
Or porters, or been ruthless enough to eat the dogs
When food ran low. If such explorers have seen
In their delirium an angel whose wings stretch
The tent flaps, there is no report of it.

The Angel Writes a Letter

I have traveled so long I do not remember the day I left or whether I was given instructions—only that the planets turned below my wings, the gears of a great engine made of darkness, and the sunlight ricocheted off the moons of Jupiter, Venus's clouds, the blue seas and green moss of Earth.

I know it is not usual for angels to write. What can we describe that you have not already seen, planned for, willed? Was it your will that sent me here: to villages where fleas outnumber the humans and dogs, to cities where the cobblestones weep and brick walls can no longer bear the weight of what they see?

I am tired of watching civilizations give way, of firing squads and mass graves, of frostbitten fingers and tree trunks shattered by gunfire. I know the vinegar smell of taverns in the morning, the sickness of prisoners whose skin bleeds from their shackles and who are afraid to look at their jailers. How heavy are the swords of conquerors, how high the pyramid of skulls, how terrified their horses....

Before, I shared your eternity, unchanging days, skies without weather. Here, days and nights spin in their own eternity—it makes me dizzy to watch them, to see the quick parade of birth and death, the occasional moment of understanding, the scent of pine sap, and the smoke of fireplaces.

Is this what I was sent to see: how flesh ages and decays, how the mind, ephemeral as music, falters and forgets, how glaciers melt and slide into the ocean?

In all that I have witnessed, I have understood so little. A boy lies in the street with a bullet hole in his forehead. His arm has fallen across another's face. Their blood pools together at the side of the road. I see each of them as they're born, eat dinner, learn to read. I remember their names and the names of their sisters and grandparents. I do not ask why I am here or how much suffering weighs compared to a star or a mountain, but perhaps I have seen enough of it. Perhaps I have been changed by this place, my wings damp with these sorrows.

As you know all things, I know this letter will reach you. I am in a village somewhere. There are mountains that are hard to cross in winter, and every night someone else dies from plague or cold.

I sit in a small tavern, writing these words and drinking a pitcher of wine. I wait patiently for your reply.

The Street That Leads to the Harbor

When the angel of sorrow walks down the street that leads to the
harbor, no one sees him.

He stops and peers into shop windows like a tourist, but he is not
looking for a wool jacket or a television. He wants to learn
what people are buying and selling and how much of their
lives they are willing to exchange for a new set of dishes or a
machine that lets them speak with other machines.

In former times, they bought mostly horses or cattle, a new blade
for the plough, a length of colored cloth to tailor a dress, or a
sharp knife for protection. Now, the angel spends a long time
outside the pharmacy—so many illnesses and so many cures.

At the café, he overhears a conversation about the war on the
other side of the border. There are cities where buildings left
standing are an anomaly, and where only the residents too
old to leave remain.

The same residents shrug. They say they do not live in the city
that has been destroyed but in the one they remember.

The angel understands because when he walks down the street
that leads to the harbor, it is no different from that walled
street that led to the Piraeus, the sloping path to the Tiber, or
the streets of Paris before Napoleon when the Seine would
flood its banks.

The people speaking in the café do not know what world's been
washed away and what world remains. The women and men
beyond the border sit on the rubble of apartment buildings
and government offices, share whatever they have for lunch,
and talk about how the grocer on the corner overcharges for
apples and flour. They suspect also that he tampers with his
scales.

If the angel heard this conversation, he would understand it. If he
heard them speaking, he would tell them they were right.

The Philosopher and the Angel

Even for the angel, finding the philosopher's house is not easy.

Everyone assumes he lives in a lodge in the forest or an apartment near the university.

In the cafés, waiters tell stories about how he will set up shop at a table in the back and spend hours in conversation with his students. For this reason, they believe he lives nearby, but no one knows which street or house.

At the university, it's the same. Occasionally, he is seen on his way to class or coming back from class, and someone remembers that once every few weeks he stops by to pick up his salary. Others say he sends a student to get it or a woman who might be his wife or his daughter.

The angel learns that none of these stories is right.

The philosopher lives in a small house not far from the railroad tracks that run to the southeast. His father had been an engineer, and the son remembers the smell of diesel on his clothes at dinner and traveling with him once all the way to Berlin.

The house looks much like others in the neighborhood. There is a garden, but no one has tended it in a long time, and when by accident it produces some tomatoes or beans, the crows and rabbits eat them before the garden's owner knows they exist.

When the angel appeared at his door, what the philosopher could not understand was why the angel had gone to the trouble to find him.

Everything I am, he said, I have put into my books. You, of all beings, know how brief our lives are and how much the same. I and my neighbor shop at the same grocery, buy the same cans of soup, and if sometimes I buy oranges or bananas from a country near the equator or read a journal he'd find boring, it's of little consequence. We are more alike than different.

The angel was seated on a worn sofa next to a cat that found neither philosopher nor angel worth a stare or twitch of her ears.

The angel smiled at the cat and respectfully disagreed. If I spoke with your neighbor, he would be at pains to tell me how unusual he was, whether it was his taste in coffee or a disease that runs in his family. He'd be certain of his difference. You are not.

It is my nature, the angel explained, to be drawn to grief and loss, to listen to the kind of story your neighbor will tell when memory fails and he thinks his dead sister has sent him on an errand. Your grief, though, is not the same as his. You have lost as much as he has, and you know how fragile your world is, the cruelty and stupidity it contains. How is it your grief is without despair?

The philosopher poured tea for himself and the angel. Spinoza, he said, would've put it better than I can. His lungs were raw from the glass he ground to make a living. He was dying, even excommunicated, but he was not unhappy.

You say you are drawn to loss. I am drawn to this house that needs to be painted, to rugs my mother took outside to clean, the dust flying off in all directions, and to my books on these shelves, some I know I'll never open again, some I will take down as soon as you've left. This is a life, such as it is, and I am satisfied with it.

They finished their tea without speaking more.

II. What the Saint Refused

The Saint of Unbelievers

The saint of unbelievers does not listen to prayers.

Neither does he convey them to the angels or higher powers.

He lives a modest, reclusive life, making baskets to be sold by village children.

Their mothers send him bread on the days they bake and something for dinner on holidays.

When the winemaker is done with a barrel, he pours off the lees and drops a bottle beside the door of the saint's cottage.

If you go to visit, do not expect him to pray with you or even to talk.

His vows do not include silence, but he has no patience with guests.

They either want something from him or want to be able to brag that they spoke with him.

If you wish to impress the saint of unbelievers, ignore him as you pass or he passes.

Choose that moment to look at your watch and say in a loud voice, "I didn't realize it was so late already."

The saint may shake his head at your foolishness, but at least he will not curse you or cause others to do so.

If this happens more than once, the saint may decide you are worth a moment's examination.

He may turn and look, first at your feet. What kind of shoes are you wearing? Is this, he may wonder, one who walks far and sees much?

Then, he will consider your hands. What kind of work does this one do? He disdains hands without callouses.

Rarely, he will consider a face, the line of the mouth, the set of the eyes. Like an Athenian, he trusts physiognomy, but unlike the Athenians, he does not trust the beautiful, the symmetrical, or the pure.

He prefers faces that like Socrates's show the gamut of vices in their gaze.

Above all, do not pretend to a virtuous expression. Those, he hates worse than cankers.

One day, a child asked him what miracles he'd performed. Shouldn't a saint perform miracles, heal the sick or bring the dead back to life, perhaps bring rain in a drought?

The saint laughed as though the child had told a joke with no understanding of its meaning.

The saint replied it was a miracle that he had not boxed the child's ears and continued laughing as he walked away.

The presence of the saint makes the priests uneasy. They fear he is judging them, sending reports to heaven.

But the saint has no interest in chatting with the holy. He also has no interest in chatting with those who aspire to be holy.

A day's walk from the saint's cottage is a town with a railroad station and a library.

The librarian there is a freethinker, which is to say that while he does not think well, he does think broadly.

This pleases the saint so that on days when the weather is good, he will visit the library, joke with the librarian, and threaten a blessing.

Passersby claim to hear the two of them laughing.

TO BELIEVE IN NOTHING

The saint of unbelievers knows it's not easy
To believe in nothing. Humans are by nature
Trusting creatures. Perhaps it is their long infancy,
The large hands of their parents, the reassuring
Heartbeats, the mother's bosom extended
To their lips. Humans, he says, dwell in a past
They're unable to put behind them. The saint,
However, has noticed they do not fool themselves
Entirely. They know that if they fail to plant
Potatoes and grain, they will starve in the winter.
If they do not take shelter, they will freeze
In the cold mountain nights. They are smart
Enough not to test God too often. The saint, though,
Trusts nothing and believes in nothing. He
Provides for himself, but only as much
As necessary. To amass wealth more than
A sack of oats that has started to mold is to risk
Believing in wealth's protection. The same
Risk applies to a house or a barn. The hut
Where the saint lives is old, and there are gaps
In the wood where the wind sings and ice
Forms on the wall. It is comforting for him
When water drips from a rafter, but it is
Not the comfort of belief. It's only
The momentary confirmation of fact,
Of a life that doesn't require his belief.
Once, he found the frozen carcass of a deer,
A buck with antlers showing that it had
Survived other winters. The saint salvaged
What he could and left the rest for foxes
And mice. But afterwards, he was troubled.
Is the knowledge of death itself a kind of belief?

The Dust of Books

The saint of unbelievers does not read poetry.
The librarian first tried to interest him in Rilke and Trakl,
Then Milosz, but he was unsuccessful. So many words,
Said the saint, and for what purpose? The librarian
Mounted a strong defense, replying that poetry broke
Through smug certainties, opened the reader
To realities beyond changing flat tires and pressing
The keys of a cash register. The saint shook his head.
The librarian, he said, had spent too long at the university
Breathing the dust of books, drinking coffee, and chewing
On the stubs of pencils. Reality is the cow bellowing
When the calf is twisted inside her, her blood mixed
With straw on the ground, and the farmer's wife left
To do the butchering, the farmer drunk in the pasture.
Reality, he said, is a cough, a fever, moving
Through a village or the cold slums of a city,
Confusion on the faces of the dying. The librarian
Struggled as he listened. He asked if there was nothing
Worth preserving, worth remembering? The saint shook
His head no, and the librarian stared at an old stain
On the floor, books waiting to be reshelved. The most
Words can do, said the saint, is remind us of the clouded
Eyes of rabbits sideways in the snow or the cries
Of a shopgirl crushed by the weight of her employer's
Belly, held by his arms, his hand over her mouth.
Then, they do have a purpose, answered the librarian.
Such as it is, acknowledged the saint.

The Saint of Unbelievers Visits the City

No one knows why he chose this particular time to go or this particular destination, only that one day he boarded a train bound for the capital. Perhaps he found a ticket someone had lost on the platform as they rushed to get a seat, or perhaps the stationmaster had given him the ticket as a joke.

The train's conductor spoke with an odd accent and knew nothing of the saint, his reputation for cursing at guests, or his anger at those who sought to please him. The conductor made the mistake of asking this strange man where he was from and what he planned to do in the city. The conductor was likely just trying to be polite. It was a long trip, and he may have been bored.

The saint replied that it was none of his concern. Did the conductor really get paid for punching little holes in tickets? Wasn't he ashamed to be so useless? The conductor brushed a speck of lint from the lapel of his blue jacket, corrected the tilt of his hat, and was about to tell the saint to take a bath next time before boarding his train. But, something stopped him. It was only a feeling for sure. The saint didn't curse, threaten him, or even look up at him. The feeling, though, made the conductor very uncomfortable. He drew back his shoulders as if he'd just delivered a sharp reply—even though he hadn't—and walked down the aisle a bit faster than usual.

The saint looked out the window. The train struggled to drag itself up hills and across the floors of valleys. When they passed villages, there were signs for garages and advertisements for beer and brands of chocolate. At night, he could see into the windows of houses. A room was lit by the glow of a television, and he saw a silhouette of heads turned toward the light.

A woman who was travelling with two children opened a bag with food. She did not exactly recognize the saint, but he seemed familiar, so she sent the oldest child over with an apple and a broken piece of cheese. The child put them on the seat next to him and ran back. The saint ate them, including the core and the cheese rind. Then he slept.

When they arrived in the capital, it was still dark. The smell of coffee from a kiosk settled along the platform. There were porters and carts, but the saint did not travel with a suitcase. He looked first down the track in the direction from which they'd just come, then down the track the other way, toward the exit sign and a large hall filled with benches. The movement of the travelers pulled him along with them, and soon he was walking on a sidewalk that ended in a large square.

This was the historic center of the city. The buildings held all the mechanisms of government, the offices of important clerks, the senate, and at the other end of the square, the presidential palace. Sunlight was angling between the buildings, and guards were unlocking the entrances. Black automobiles carrying government ministers parked by the steps. The saint did not stop to look at any of this.

He walked directly to the presidential palace and climbed the steps toward the ornately carved doors that separated it from the street. At the top of the stairs, two guards stopped him and asked what business he had there. When the saint did not answer them, one of the guards grew impatient and lifted his rifle butt up to his chest as though to push the saint away, but the other was fresh from the country and had better manners. He explained to the saint that they asked because the most important man in the nation lived here and that everyone's welfare depended on the decisions he made. The saint nodded his head and demanded to meet him.

At this, both guards laughed and were moving to send him on his way when the president himself appeared. He had finished his breakfast, lingered over an extra cup of coffee, and on impulse had decided to surprise certain senators with his unannounced presence shortly before a crucial vote. He looked at the saint and with a smile he had practiced for years asked, "Who is this?"

The saint replied that this was a question he had been trying to answer for a long time. "One day," he said, "I realized the problem was the question itself." Then, before the president could move on, he continued, "Now I have a question as well. How many wives, mistresses, and fat children do you have that you require such a large house?"

The saint was imprisoned for the next two months while the public prosecutor and the court decided what to do with him. Fortunately, the story of his conversation with the president circulated throughout the capital, and the opposition secured his release under the misconception that he was a political activist.

Upon discovering their mistake in the course of an unpleasant interview only disclosed to party leadership, officials in charge of such things quickly dispatched an assistant to the minister of transportation to purchase one 3rd class ticket and make sure the saint boarded the next train back to his village.

The Voice of God

One night the pope had a dream. In the dream, the voice of God told him about a saint who lived in a village to the North, and when the pope woke up, he understood that he had been charged with finding this saint.

The pope assigned three priests to the task. One was a skilled diplomat, one an expert in church law, and the third was a trusted friend he'd known for many years. They began by looking for reports of miracles, but there were none. They also looked for reports of heroism and sacrifice. A man in France had climbed up the side of a building to save a child hanging from a balcony, but he turned out to be a Muslim. They combed as well through newspaper articles about wars and bombings, thinking that a saint would likely emerge in such a setting.

All their efforts came to nothing until they sent letters to each parish, asking for reports regarding anyone who appeared to be or was treated as a saint. They received several replies. In Czechoslovakia, a woman cured burns with prayer, and in Germany, an old man had been seen flying. Both were investigated and found to be questionable.

There was, however, a certain individual in a remote village who was reputed to be a saint, but the priest who reported him could not point to anything he had done that would evidence sainthood. Because they were embarrassed at having had so little success, all three investigators decided to travel to the village.

The journey took place during the hottest part of the summer and was quite uncomfortable. The mountain roads were in disrepair, and they had to stop the car, which had a bad exhaust, so the expert in church law could throw up in the bushes.

In the village, they were met with more discomfort. There was no hotel or inn where they could stay. There was nothing in the vicinity that tourists wanted to see, and the local population did not have a reputation for hospitality. The investigators slept on wooden benches in the church. The priest who had written to them had died from a stroke after walking a great distance in the heat, and the village could not decide whose responsibility it was to receive them.

For dinner, they ate only the bread and sausage they'd purchased on their way to the village, and exhaustion left them eager to sleep even on benches. That night, all three dreamed the same dream. They were walking to the outskirts of the village where boulders had piled up from landslides in some distant geologic past. The mountain rose sharply before them, and they saw a cottage, more accurately a hut, on the far side of the boulders and the figure of a man surrounded in light.

The next day, they went out to find the man they had seen. They walked south, where the village ended, and they saw the boulders and the steep slope of the mountain. They also found the hut, but the man illuminated in the dream was not at home. Each day, they came back to the dwelling, but he did not appear.

The diplomat was unperturbed. He told the others stories of how much patience had been required when he negotiated with presidents and warlords. The expert in church law agreed and only regretted that he did not have access to a proper library where he might find a precedent for evaluating such a situation. The third was largely silent but implied that his own patience was much more limited.

When the investigators finally discovered the man they were looking for, he was trading baskets he'd woven for a sack of grain and some bacon. He was not illuminated as he had been in the dream, and he was cursing the shopkeeper for underestimating the value of his baskets. The investigators immediately offered to pay for any supplies the man might need, but he rejected their charity even more rudely than the shopkeeper's negotiation.

They returned to Rome more confused than ever. Soon afterwards, the old pope died, and a new one was elected. He too dreamed of the basket-weaving recluse and heard the voice of God describe him as a saint. The new pope summoned the three investigators, and they repeated the report they'd given to his predecessor. There was no evidence of sainthood, only the dreams and the voice of God.

The new pope considered all this and stated that God must have his reasons, unfathomable as they may be. At the same time, to declare this disagreeable man a saint could be a source of great embarrassment. He decided to do what all good leaders, secular and religious, are best at: he compromised. He sent word to the local church authorities to send reports back each year on the basket-maker, observing closely for miraculous events, and in the meantime, to treat the man as a saint even though he would not be officially recognized as such.

Far away, in a village to the north, a basket-maker woke up from a dream laughing.

During the War

War Comes to the Village

A truck filled with soldiers parked in front of the church. Another truck, an empty one, pulled up behind it.

Even though the village was hard to reach, everyone had already heard about the war. The president and the senate, angry at a threat made by a neighbor to the north, had declared war and mobilized the reserves.

However, the country had no reserves, so the senate passed a law declaring all males between the ages of 14 and 67 to be reservists in the nation's army.

While a surprising number of villagers were herding sheep and cows in the mountains that day, the soldiers did manage to find several reservists, including the saint of unbelievers.

When a certain captain grabbed him by the shoulder, the saint's protest took the form of invective accusing the captain's mother of improprieties with bus drivers and mailmen.

Despite the mayor's intervention, the saint, unconscious from a beating, was carried to the truck waiting with its engine still running.

The driver was unsure it would start again if he switched it off.

The Conscript

Some men are not intended to be soldiers.

When the saint woke up, he was freezing from a bucket of water poured on his head and aching from the bruises the captain's boots had left on his ribs.

Someone handed him a uniform that was far too large for him, but at least it was dry.

Later, he noticed a small hole almost in line with the buttons of the jacket and another just below the shoulders.

The saint was not issued a rifle, but that had nothing to do with his personality or any suspicion that he would not make good use of it.

The army had run out of rifles three days earlier and knives a day after that.

But, a clever officer, who before the war managed a bicycle factory, had the solution: reservists without weapons would storm the enemy lines barehanded, an act of courage sure to strike terror into the opposing ranks.

Any reservist who retreated or failed to attack would be shot by troops coming up behind him.

The officer regarded his plan as perfect strategy.

The saint regarded it as marginally preferable to being poisoned by the sour-smelling soup that caused cramps and a sudden rush to the latrines.

Before dawn, the order came to attack, the reservists moved forward, and the saint stumbled on the road along with the rest.

Like most of the others, he had no intention of killing anyone. He already understood that the war was a kind of insanity, and he should get away as soon as he could.

The Hero

At the first sound of rifle fire and mortar rounds, an officer ordered the troops into some woods.

They waited, unsure of where the enemy was or where they were.

Once, a deer broke cover. In the dark, it sounded like a horse or men running.

Luckily, no one had weapons, or they would have shot each other in panic.

The saint moved his back against a large tree and slid down to rest. When he woke up, it was already morning.

His platoon was gone, and although he could smell gunpowder and smoke, no one was firing.

The saint considered that this might be a good time to begin his walk back to the mountains and began retracing his steps.

There was a small stream by the road that he didn't remember. Now, it was filled with bodies in uniform, and the water rose over and around their cold faces and arms.

The saint recognized some, and some had different colored jackets. There was nothing to be done, and he walked past them.

He heard the sound of brakes behind him, and an officer shouted, "Identify yourself."

The saint replied that he was not among the dead.

At headquarters, several officers asked him questions at once, so that he found it difficult to answer any of them.

Finally, a sergeant explained that the saint was the only survivor of the attack and that no one knew what had happened.

A tall man with gold braid and stars approached him.

The sergeant pushed the saint to stand up, and the officer informed him he was now a hero of the republic and pinned a silver medal on his chest.

The saint carefully unpinned the medal and examined it. Then, he threw it on the muddy floor and walked outside.

Strangely, no one tried to stop him.

The Saint and the Gamblers

The saint of unbelievers rarely meets gamblers.

He lives near a village in the mountains, not in a spa or noisy metropolis.

His neighbors, to the extent he has neighbors, are farmers, and if they bet, it is only on the spring rains or the grain ripening in autumn.

No one buys lottery tickets, and the horses on their farms are not suitable for racing.

The saint himself doesn't think much of gamblers.

They believe in luck and in the excitement that hovers over each card, each spin of the wheel.

The saint, if questioned, would have shaken his head and asked, "This luck you speak of, can you show it to me? If this is something you own, can you sell it to me?" But, no one is foolish enough to speak with the saint about such topics.

Even the librarian who lives in the next town by the railway line knows better than to mention such a subject.

He did ask the saint once whether Dante was right to place gamblers in hell, and the saint's reply was that it was as good as anywhere else to place them.

The librarian was not surprised by his answer.

Don't think that the saint has never met gamblers. When he was younger, before he settled in his cabin outside the village, he traveled south as far as Spain and Italy.

Gamblers there bragged to him of the fortunes they'd lost and made, especially lost. They didn't care, they'd say, about money—it was only something to wager.

Admittedly, this attitude interested the saint. He also cared very little for money and was surprised there were others who felt the same.

But, unlike the gamblers he met, the saint had no interest in the thrill of winning or of losing.

Money was not important enough to desire or to disdain.

When he accuses the shopkeeper of cheating him, it's only because he's amused by how the man's face grows flushed, his fingers grip the counter, and how quick he is to swear he's done no such thing.

The saint is also amused that the villagers are frightened of his curses.

The saint, however, takes certain gamblers seriously. He despises Pascal's wager, and when he argues with the librarian, he says the Frenchman was a poor gambler who could only see two outcomes and did not consider what he had lost in the betting.

The librarian asked him if all men, including himself, were not gamblers, wagering their short lives on this or that purpose.

The saint poured himself more of the librarian's excellent tea, and replied, "It is even worse than you imagine. We all wager, as you say, on one purpose or another, on tending a farm or reading philosophy, on becoming a soldier, a priest, or an electrician, but regardless what we wager or how long we live, we never discover if we were right."

The Saint Sometimes Misses Belief

Although he would be reluctant to admit it, the saint of unbelievers sometimes misses belief.

Not for the usual reasons, though—he's not afraid of dying, and he stopped looking for purpose in the world when he was still an adolescent.

What the saint regrets are the conversations he might have had, interrogating the right or wrong of his own actions and those of others, how he might have justified living as he does, how he would have responded to the interlocutor who says nothing but whose silence is both question and answer.

As it is, he makes do with the sounds he hears at night in his cabin, the shrieks of owls, the wind cracking a tree limb in winter, the muffled thump of snow sliding off the roof.

In the mountains where he lives, there are spots where he can look down on a village or town, not much different from the toy railroads constructed by children. Belief, he thinks, is like these views, full of certainty that the place he observes is what it purports to be. From the top of a mountain, the various pieces fit together so easily: the store across the main street from the train station, the schoolhouse and the church, the brothel and tavern. From the top of a mountain, everything looks symmetrical. From here, it would be easy to imagine the lives of villagers moving like the automatons of medieval clocks. At the same time each day, the baker will stand outside the glass door of his shop and stare in at the oven and the brown loaves of hard-crusted bread on the counter.

The saint knows that this view from a great height is completely wrong. The baker's wife hides the bruises on her face. The librarian tells him that the baker's children have similar bruises, and they never stop by anymore to turn the pages of a book. The saint knows that pain is never symmetrical, and he refuses to pretend that the pieces fit together.

It is no accident, he thinks—and it is only a thought because he has learned to do without an interlocutor—that prophets and philosophers have been so fond of mountaintops. They remind him of the hikers he has seen from time to time. They wear short pants and boots and carry ridiculously large bags on their backs. They climb to the top of this or that peak and then, full of achievement, back down to the village and the train station.

Whatever they think they have learned will disappoint them.

Museums

The librarian expressed surprise that the saint had visited museums. There are no museums in the mountains, and the saint had never expressed an interest in painting or sculpture. The baskets he sold in the village were sturdy and well-shaped but had nothing artful about them. Moreover, the saint expressed little but disdain for novels and poems, and even the essays of Montaigne failed to receive his approval.

Surely, these paintings that hang in the Louvre and the Prado require belief, the librarian argued. Not at all, the saint replied. When I stand before a Velázquez, I do not think, how real are these children, the frowning dwarf, and the thick-furred dog falling asleep in the foreground. I see the painter at his canvas and the man departing up the staircase in a mirror, and I nod my head involuntarily. Velázquez and I are sharing a joke. He is like the traveling magician whose truck arrives each year in the village. My neighbors buy tickets, and red scarves appear in the air. A woman disappears from one box and reappears in another. Some of them still gape at the empty box, but most see the trick for what it is.

The librarian finished his tea and asked the saint why human beings had made these images of what they saw, perhaps even before they lived in houses or learned to cook their food. The saint did not need to deliberate. If they could make a picture of it, he said, then it became more real to them. People are born without a story. Images of themselves, of their animals and their parents, and anything else that comes to mind, give them a story they can believe. But the longer they make such images, the less they believe the stories they tell. Finally, they build museums, great buildings filled with stories no one believes.

When I traveled in my youth, I would spend all day in the hallways and galleries. In the summer, I would feel the cool marble of stairs and columns; in winter, the ice and wind did not penetrate their walls. In a museum, no one bothers you with stupid conversations. No one asks where you're from or how long you're staying in Madrid. In a church, someone will see your torn jacket and, wishing to think well of themselves, will come up to offer *encouragement*. In a museum, that never happens. The paintings would not allow it. There is something about a museum that makes such gestures embarrassing. Surrounded by thousands of flat surfaces, each its own world, people usually retreat into themselves. This is a relief for those of us who do not crave their company.

TEMPTATION

The saint of unbelievers believes in nothing, especially not in himself.

If he resists temptation, it is only because the usual objects of temptation don't interest him much. He has no taste for delicacies or other pleasures, and human beings are a burden he prefers to avoid.

He sleeps on a mat covering a sack stuffed with straw, and in winter he covers himself with a second such sack. Pieces of straw stick out from the weave and scratch red welts on his back and sides. He has learned to ignore them.

He ignores as well his beard and hair growing long and unkept, and for clothes, he wears whatever he has been given.

Years before, children from the village would throw dried cow turds at him as he walked by the houses and low buildings, but he would only pick them up and stuff them in his bag to keep the fire going at night.

There was a young priest who invited him to preach at the church, but he declined. It is a hard enough occupation to be a saint who believes in nothing without having to explain himself to those who will not understand anyway.

In the summer, in the evenings, he lies outside in a field and stares up at the stars and moon wheeling across the sky. This is how he tests himself.

He says to the sky, "You want us to think you are an order encompassing everything, but you are full of accidents, of falling stars, and the dust of planets destroyed by time. You are not worth belief."

It is the only temptation that matters.

Blasphemy

The saint of unbelievers does not understand blasphemy.
He also does not bother with blasphemy. Last spring,
A visiting priest gave a sermon in the town square. He warned
The villagers against licentious books and films, referring
To them as "blasphemous droppings from the bowels of Satan."
The saint admired his language and decided to use the expression
The next time he cursed a tradesman. However, he also
Thought it was a silly speech because the villagers rarely
Read books, of any kind, and there was no audience that
Would make the screening of films profitable. The word
Blasphemy though was a different matter. To the saint,
It suggested speech that was an affront to a deity or religion.
He thought for a moment whether any speech could
Offend an unbeliever. He, for example, was not offended
By the words of the priest. It was not clear to him either
Why the priest's church should be troubled by new stories
That were not so different from stories of antiquity. This is
Not to say he cared about them at all, only he had yet
To find anything that offended him. In the fall,
The priest returned. His audience was smaller because
He came during the last days of harvest. This time
The saint was also occupied, patching some—but not all—
Of the holes in his roof. In the afternoon, he walked
Into the village to see if anyone was throwing away
Something useful. To his surprise, he heard the priest
Encourage his handful of listeners to search the villagers'
Homes, seeking out a comprehensive list of sinful books
And devices, some of which even the saint had never
Heard of. He imagined the grocer and his wife, who were
Listening carefully, making use of these items, and he
Began to laugh so hard he almost fell over. This did not
Escape the notice of the priest. This priest was not
Acquainted with the saint and urged the crowd to
Attack and silence the blasphemer. It quickly
Became clear that the saint was not the only one
Confused about blasphemy. The villagers looked
At each other for a moment and started to wander away.

This caused the saint to wonder: *perhaps they were not Nearly as stupid as he'd always imagined them.* He made A note to discuss this with the librarian.

When the Saint Was Dying

In one of their conversations, the saint of unbelievers argued to the librarian that Socrates was an actor who'd turned his death into a performance, complete with an audience of his students. The saint preferred Aristotle who, without applause, left Athens to prevent a similar drama.

When the saint himself was dying, he told no one, but the news spread quickly anyway.

Villagers whispered to each other and then to the inhabitants of nearby towns.

By the time the librarian heard, the saint was no longer able to leave his makeshift bed. Villagers brought him food that he was largely unable to eat.

The new priest came to visit as well. He was unacquainted with the saint and only heard that storekeepers were frightened of his outbursts. Even though he was unable to get up, the saint still summoned the strength to insult the priest and send him away shocked that a dying man could curse so vividly.

The same day, the librarian crossed the mountain and arrived in the afternoon.

He boiled water over a small fire, portioned out some tea leaves, and held a cup up to the saint's lips.

The saint was pleased that the librarian didn't feel the need to speak. If they'd spoken, the saint might have had to reassure the librarian that he didn't fear what was happening to him. But they did not speak. They only drank tea and stared at the fire.

Although the librarian had never visited the saint before, the cabin was much as he'd pictured it. A broom stood propped up against the wall, and drafts from the roof and door pulled the fire one way, then another. In the corner, there was a rusted lantern, but no oil.

The librarian made himself dinner from some bread and cheese he'd brought in his bag.

He broke off a piece of the bread and tried, unsuccessfully, to get the saint to eat.

He also covered the saint with the closest thing to a blanket he could find, a stiff animal skin, something the saint had probably found on a walk.

The odor of the saint's sickness was suspended in the air like smoke.

The next morning, when he saw the saint was no longer breathing, the librarian did exactly what the dead man would have done in his place. He closed the door of the cabin and walked home.

George Franklin is the winner of the 2023 Yeats Poetry Prize. His book *Remote Cities* is his third full-length poetry collection with Sheila-Na-Gig Editions, complementing *Noise of the World* (2020) and *Traveling for No Good Reason* (winner of the Sheila-Na-Gig Editions manuscript competition in 2018). He has also authored the dual-language collection, *Among the Ruins / Entre las ruinas* (translated by Ximena Gómez and published by Katakana Editores, 2020), and a chapbook, *Travels of the Angel of Sorrow* (Blue Cedar Press, 2020). He is the co-translator, along with the author, of Ximena Gómez's *Último día / Last Day* and co-author with Gómez of *Conversaciones sobre agua / Conversations About Water* (Katakana Editores 2019 & 2023). He practices law in Miami.

Also by George Franklin
at Sheila-Na-Gig Editions

REMOTE CITIES
ISBN: 9798985524277
$17.00 ($4.00 US Shipping per order)

From a cathedral in Cuernavaca with its frescos of samurai and soon-to-be-martyred priests to neighborhoods in Miami at the end of lockdown, to New York City in the 1970s, or to mythic Greece, the poems in *Remote Cities* are conscious of history as a process happening right now. They look back at us with an urgency that demands response, not that we embrace this or that political or religious dogma but that we live our lives with a sense of their fragility and value.

PRAISE FOR REMOTE CITIES:

The poems in George Franklin's *Remote Cities* are poems for grown-ups, for people who know what it is to have loved, to have been disappointed in love, to have recovered love. They are wise, thoughtful, self-effacing, realistic about nature and human nature, without illusion but also without bitterness. They understand what it is to find one's self embedded among the complex ties of family and family history, with all its unsolved issues of duty and responsibility. They understand, without posing and without extenuation, what it is to live in a fallen political and historical world in which there are few unmixed institutions and few soluble problems. They see human life in the widest context, as they are reflected in history, poetry, fine art, and the way the classic stories face us with but do not solve the dark puzzle of our being. To all of these George Franklin brings an acute eye for detail, and a sad, knowing, and thoughtful sense of what it is to be alive and to know that life all the way through.
—John Burt, author of *Victory*

If Robert Hass was right, in that all the new thinking about loss resembles the old thinking, what can be done to restore our lives and world? *Remote Cities* gathers the lost tribes, from antiquity to modernity to now, in a collection ritually anchored by the presence and body of the beloved, "mi amor": her nightgown, white shoulders, and the memories, walks, and sensuous meals they share. Reminding us that every person, poem, era, and artwork is also looking back at the perceiver, Franklin has done the heretofore impossible: write an epic love poem that, in its refusal of death and dying, casts a new narrative song on the world's "utter wreck," making stars shine brighter than before.

—Virginia Konchan, author of *Bell Canto*

NOISE OF THE WORLD

ISBN: 9781735400204
$17.00 ($4.00 US Shipping per order)

The poems in *Noise of the World* tell real stories, real because the poet doesn't shy away from the limitations of being human. There are love poems, moments of desire, of "Pressing my lips and teeth hard against / Your shoulder, dissolving beneath your / Fingers, tongue, the shiver in your / Abdomen," but they are tempered by the knowledge that the person loved will never be fully known and, ultimately, even desire is something that can't be understood. His poems of history, like his love poems, find their reality in particular moments such as "The dark hands of the Zapatistas / Curled around white cups, eyes ignoring / The camera," or "That cup of coffee and the soft, white bread / Depend on being born here, not there. Then, / Not some other time." History encompasses as well the poet's family, his life in Miami with his compañera, the Colombian poet Ximena Gómez, the classes he teaches in Florida prisons, his travels to Europe, Colombia, and Mexico, the Covid-19 quarantine, the writers and artists who've shaped how he sees and responds, and the solitude he experiences: the "House that quiet, the dog outside poking / His nose into opossum smells or / The pleasure of rotting leaves."

This book celebrates sensual life and the imagination while reminding us that even in moments of love or solitude, even when we don't hear it, the noise of the world is still there.

PRAISE FOR NOISE OF THE WORLD:

With his new and remarkable collection, George Franklin offers vivid images, portraits, snapshots, and narratives, conjuring the wonder of travel and romance, the bewilderments of aging and loss, the treasures and illusions of selfhood, and the complex legacies of family. These poems are meticulously crafted, Franklin addressing what it means to love, to be aware of inevitable death, and to seek wholeness in, as he writes, "the random pieces of our lives." Impeccable work from a versatile poet at the height of his alchemical powers.

—John Amen, Editor, *Pedestal Magazine*

In his new collection *Noise of the World*, George Franklin offers an intimate exploration of the emotional pressure points in our lives. In this day and age when the loudness of life can overwhelm, his careful observation of people and places, in memory and recollection, in imagining and re-imagining, focuses us on the importance of who we are and what we do in the unseen moments of our days. The subtle power of Franklin's craft lies in the attention and intention, and at times devotion, of his words, which resonate long after reading. Threaded through this collection is a deep understanding of the connections between us and the tenuous nature of it all. *Noise of the World* chronicles a lifetime of tender observation, whether it is a connection with places traveled to or home during lock-down, or in moments in time with a lover, an aging self, or a dying father. These deftly crafted poems slow down time, allowing us to savour the moments that our lives are made of.

—Kusi Okamura, Editor, *The Wild Word*

TRAVELING FOR NO GOOD REASON

Winner: 2018 Sheila-Na-Gig Editions Poetry Manuscript contest
ISBN: 9781732940604
$17.00 —($4.00 US Shipping per order)

These poems in *Traveling for No Good Reason* tell stories, and they invite the reader to enter into those stories. Whether the poet is drinking Cuban coffee in Miami, visiting Joseph Brodsky's grave in Venice, teaching writing workshops in a Florida prison, learning to read Greek in New York City in the 1980s, or trying to make sense out of a love that is unexpected and undeserved, the stories are about the recompense we receive for our losses, the pleasures and ideas that allow us to start to live all over again. Sometimes that recompense is erotic, sometimes merely the fact of telling the story. The poems are conversational in style while at the same time seeking out what is often hard to talk about: the end of a marriage, a friend's slow death, or what desire might actually mean. Regardless, it's the conversation that's always foremost. In looking to understand, these poems themselves want to be understood, to be transparent. They may engage historical or mythological figures or the woman whose life the poet shares, but their conversation is ultimately with the reader.

Sheila-Na-Gig Editions

www.ingramcontent.com/pod-product-compliance
Lightning Source LLC
Chambersburg PA
CBHW061324120626
46546CB00007B/2666